AF583353

Anzac Day Parade

When Anzac Day Parade *was first concieved, the authors were assisted by:*
Rose Young, Auckland War Memorial Museum;
Gary Walker, Papakura RSA;
Chris Swift, photographer;
and Crete veteran Noel Dromgool and his wife, Peggy.
Noel and Peggy have since passed away.
May they rest in peace.

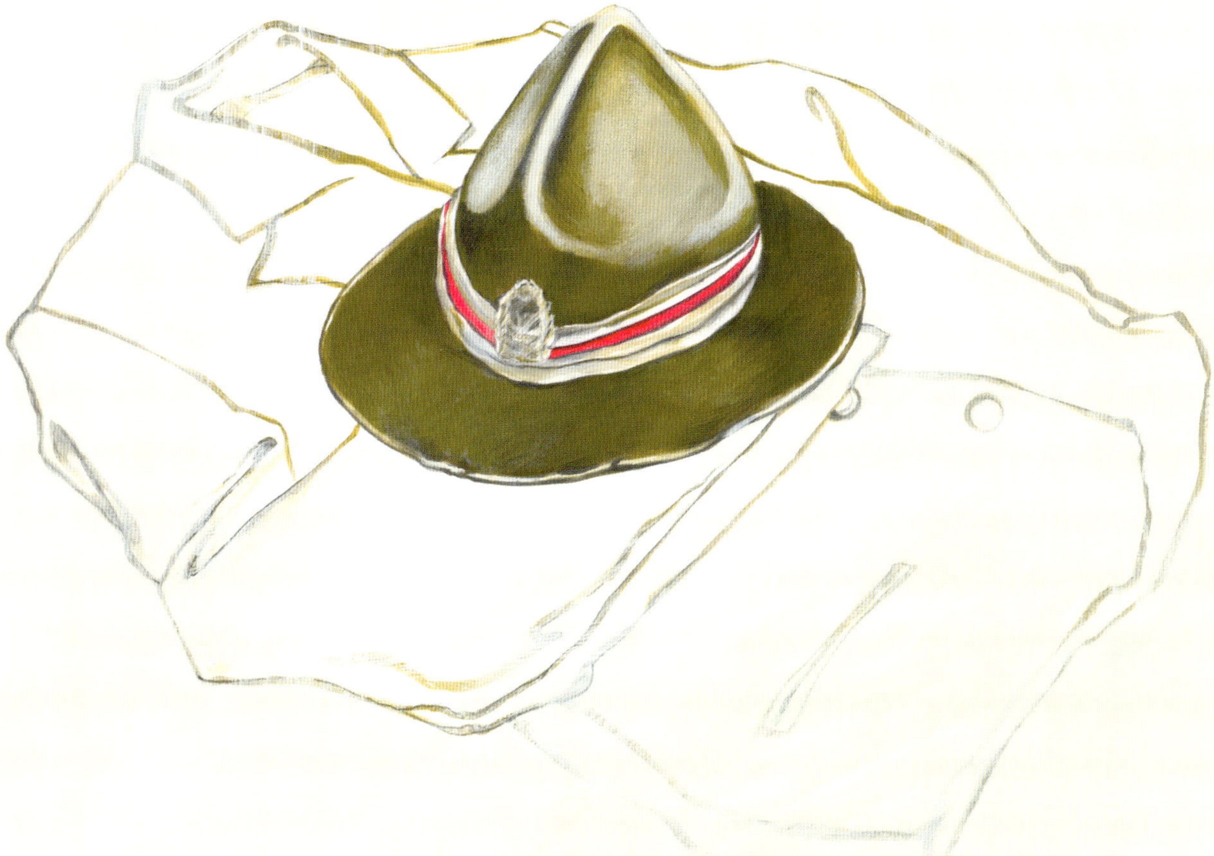

Anzac Day Parade

Glenda Kane & Lisa Allen

There he stood on the sun-parched hill,
a straggler from 18th Battalion.

A chest-load of medals, a leg full of shrapnel;
that's what he got for his valiance.

So many years since he saw the battle
when ninety-three mates got blown away
by cracking mortar and machine gun rattle,

now names on a plaque at the RSA.

TO OUR GALLANT
LEST WE FORG
R.STOCKTO
F.A.STRACH
A.STUART
G.D.STUBBS
P.STUBBS
J.C.SWINTO
L.THOMA
B.THORLEY

Fear in their hearts, guns in their hands,
the men stood shoulder to shoulder.

One by one in that foreign land,
they became a fallen soldier.

Did ya shoot them dead?
asked the bright-eyed boy.
Did it feel real cool to kill?

With a voice bereft of joy
he sighed:
No son, it was no thrill.

The boy thought that was that, until
the old man spoke some more.

His eyes downcast to the grass on the hill,
he said: What a dirty war.

ISOLA DI CRETA

My mate, he said, as church bells pealed,
Hugh Ward, now who'd have thought it?

Standing there in a Cretan field,
old Hughie boy, he bought it.

NEW ZEALAND POST OFFICE

TELEGRA

Dear Elizabeth,

I am writing to express my deep sympathy at the loss of your brother, Hugh. I was with him at the end. He was very brave. He asked

Age won't weary him, he said,
but boy, it's wearied me.

He looked out over the young one's head
and the past was all he could see.

Now he shuffled off towards the RSA
for a glass to drown his sorrows,
and to toast the boys who've had their day

and for whom there are no tomorrows.

LET THESE PANEL

EVER BE FILLED

When German parachutists rained down on Crete early on May 20th, 1941, one of the most dramatic battles of World War II had begun. New Zealand, Australian, British and Greek troops, helped by Cretan civilians, tried to repel the German assault but, by May 26th, it became clear that retreat and evacuation was their only option.

The Battle of Crete was a heavy defeat for the Allied forces: over 3500 men were killed and 15,000 were captured.

These brave men and thousands of others are acknowledged on April 25th every year, when ANZAC Day is commemorated in Australia and New Zealand. People of all ages gather at war memorials to remember the dead and honour the living. With each passing year, the number of returned servicemen in attendance diminishes — but the number of young people increases.

At the going down of the sun and in the morning
we will remember them.

First published by Puffin Books (NZ), 2010
This edition published by David Bateman Ltd, 2022

David Bateman Ltd
Unit 2/5 Workspace Drive, Hobsonville, Auckland 0618, New Zealand
www.batemanbooks.co.nz

ISBN: 978-1-77689-014-9

Designed and illustrated by Lisa Allen
Printed in China by Toppan Leefung Printing Ltd